PRAISE FOR *IN OTHER WORDS*

Susan Rountree's observations come straight from the heart, but also straight from the shoulder: no weasel words, no smoothing or straightening of the often rough, tangled road that mothers tread as they lead their children from utter dependence to responsible adulthood. In these vignettes from her own experience, she admits her own vulnerability and doubts, as well as her adherence to principles rooted firmly in love and common sense—and good humor.

A word of advice: don't read this book straight through. Ration yourself to one or two entries at a time, then sit back and savor the warmth, the wit, the honesty, and insight which Rountree shares so generously with all of us who love children and cherish families.

SALLY BUCKNER,

AUTHOR OF *STRAWBERRY HARVEST* AND

EDITOR OF *WORD AND WITNESS: 100 YEARS OF NORTH CAROLINA POETRY*.

ALSO BY SUSAN BYRUM ROUNTREE
Nags Headers

WINNER, WILLIE PARKER PEACE HISTORY BOOK AWARD, 2001

PRAISE FOR *NAGS HEADERS*

"*Nags Headers* is the next best thing to a day at the beach"

SOUTHERN LIVING

"Rountree's collection of memorable Tar Heels provides
the tang of a mid-summer ocean breeze to her charmer."

PUBLISHER'S WEEKLY DAILY

"*Nags Headers* is the book we all had in our heads,
those of us whose flesh and bones are needed inland
but whose hearts spend endless Mays and Septembers
on those narrow shifting strips of sand...."

THE UNIVERSITY OF NORTH CAROLINA ALUMNI REVIEW

"Warm and picturesque, *Nags Headers* makes
past years come alive."

AMAZON.COM

To learn more, visit *www.nagsheaders.com*

To Sydney —
Get out your
Kleenex!

In Mother Words

Essays by Susan Byrum Rountree

May 27, 2005

CHAPEL HILL
PRESS, INC.®

The following essays appeared previously, some under different titles, in *The News & Observer*'s "Our Lives" column: "But You Just Got Here," August 21, 2002; "The Year of 'We,'" May 28, 2002; "Just the Right Music," February 5, 2002; "Shattered," June 5, 2001; "Spirit of Christmas Passed," December 11, 2001; "A Case of Senioritis," November 13, 2001; "Author Mom," July 24, 2001; "College Visits and Empty Nests," March 13, 2001.

Others first printed in *The News & Observer*: "My Shadow Seeks Her Own Sun," February 27, 2000; "Snow Fun," January 12, 1996; "My Baby, Lost & Found," September 10, 1995; "Giant Step," June 1, 1995; "I'll Never Fill Mom's Hats," May 11, 1995; "Yes, in Virginia, There Is a Santa," December 22, 1994; "For Mom, Parting Is Such Sweet Sorrow," August 23, 1992.

In Mother Words
Copyright © 2003 by Susan Byrum Rountree

Published by The Chapel Hill Press, Inc.
1829 East Franklin Street, No. 300A
Chapel Hill, NC 27514

ISBN Number 1-880849-61-5
Library of Congress Catalog Number 2003102748

Printed in the United States of America
07 06 05 04 03   10 9 8 7 6 5 4 3 2 1

For M. and G.—

It's your story, after all.

Love, Mom

Acknowledgments

Thanks to: Kristen Svingen, Dawn Ronco, David Frauenfelder, and Mary Cornazter, fine editors all, and to the members of the Borders Writer's Group, creative encouragers who never stop teaching me how to write; to Judy Goodson, who first published my writing about the little things; and to my children, for putting up with me as I put their lives down on the page.

Table of Contents

In Mother Words

MOTHER IN ME

When I gave birth to my daughter on a frigid morning in December almost twenty years ago, I thought that meant I had become a mother. A baby to rock and coo to, that's what I'd wanted for so long. But it wasn't until a few days later that my transformation occurred. It happened when my own mother, who'd come to take care of us for awhile, walked out my front door with my husband and said: "Give her a bath while I'm gone."

Now you have to know my mother to understand the power of these words. Take a bath, she was always telling me while growing up, and make it scalding. It'll serve to scrub away whatever ails you, be it headache, splinter or broken heart.

She'd been right, of course. I'd even followed her advice not four days before. Tired of being swollen and perpetually in wait, I lowered my nine-months' pregnant body into a scalding tub and sat, knowing this was exactly what my mother would advise me to do. And believe me, it soon cured what ailed me *and* my baby. A few hours later, in the middle of the night, the baby who would be named Meredith told me it was time to come into the world.

A week later, when Mama handed my daughter over to me before heading out the door, she knew full well that "Give her a bath" was code for me—her own baby girl—instructing me to take my place among the mothers of my family. It was time, not to take the bath, but give it.

Of course, I resisted. I'd watched her give Meredith a bath on the giant sponge on my tiny bathroom counter, but aside from wringing a dripping washcloth over her squirming body, I'd never been in charge. I had no idea how much baby bath to use or if I should wash her hair. Where would I put her while the water was heating up? What if it got too hot? How would I, with only two hands between me, find all the soiled places between her folds, hold her slick form without dropping her on the floor?

I heard the door slam behind me and pondered all these things in my heart. Then I stared at the pink form in my arms, realizing for the very first time, that my mother would be going home soon, and this baby was mine to keep.

As I remember this, I think about the time we'd been studying the Chinese culture in sixth grade, and I had asked my mother if I could take one of her china bowls for show and tell.

"Only if you don't break it," she said to me. So I wrapped it carefully in newspaper, put it in a paper grocery bag, and set out. That afternoon I triumphantly walked the mile home, juggling my mother's bowl and an armful of books. I made it all the way to the back door, then paused, the books and the bowl in one arm, trying to open the door handle. Need I say more? If I couldn't be trusted with a china bowl, how on earth could I be trusted with a baby?

I thought about not giving her a bath at all and just saying I did. I mean, she looked clean enough to me. But after twenty years of living under the roof of my mother, the master of bath giving, I knew full well she'd find me out.

Poor Meredith. I tried to be gentle. Her wide eyes watched as I tested the water and soaped the soft cloth. She was tiny, slippery, not six pounds, but to me she weighed sixteen. I was as careful as I knew how to be, and after a minute or two, my heart slowed a little, and I began singing to her, marveling at the very idea that this tiny form was so much a part of me.

When my mother came home that afternoon, Meredith was not only clean, but fed and burped, and I'd finally begun my journey as her mother.

Soon enough, though, you learn that when you are out in the world with your new baby, everyone becomes your mother. They are well-meaning when they tell you you're holding her the wrong way, offer advice on how to properly burp her or what to do if she won't stop crying. Sometimes their advice is worth taking.

I learned this lesson on my first trip out of the house with Meredith when we paid our initial visit to the pediatrician's office, where the waiting room is command central for mothers who claim to know more about how to raise a baby than the mother sitting next to them.

This was January, middle Georgia, and though that part of the South is better known for its gentle winters, 1984 began as the year before had ended, biting cold and blustery.

I had dressed Meredith for her first outing, a first layer of T-shirt and diapers, then a layer of tiny white tights and pink sailor dress. Next came a hooded sweater and socks. After that, a quilted snowsuit that was so big her feet didn't reach the toes. Then came a blue toboggan, bought when we thought she'd surely be a boy. The final layer was made up of two, mind you, two soft blankets.

So tightly bound was she that you could barely see her tiny face. Her body wouldn't bend in the car seat, no doubt because she'd doubled her weight in the ten minutes it had taken me to dress her. Never mind. My baby would not be catching cold in this weather.

When I reached the doctor's office, the nurses gathered around to see her. I beamed, at this most perfect creature I'd created, almost by myself.

"Take some of these covers off this baby," said one of them, surely a mother of ten. Could she tell that I'd been at it less than two weeks?

I stood back, mortified, as she began to peel the layers away from my newborn, revealing the face of a child who has loved hot weather ever since.

"Always be sure that you give her space to breathe," the nurse told me.

(If I'd tried to take Meredith out of the house when my mother was still visiting, no doubt she would have been the one to give me this advice. When I related this story to my sister, she admitted that, though her daughter was born in the middle of August, the first time she took her outside, she wrapped her accordingly. My mother, who was a witness to this folly, was quick to remove the layers from my niece, lest she have a heat stroke.)

Give her a bath; give her room to breathe. I think of my own mother and how many times she bathed me, not only in scalding water to scrub my ills away, but in the love she showered me with while I was growing up. I had no other model, and surely I didn't need one. She gave me room to breathe, too, room to learn the ropes without her looking over my shoulder every minute.

When I look back on almost twenty years of being a mother myself, I know I've tried to follow these two rules. Meredith knows all about the power of the hot bath, and though she may think I've suffocated her with my questions about her life, I hope she can appreciate those times when I've given her some needed air, allowing her to shape her own future the way she feels is right.

There may be times for each of us when, as daughters, we are asked to mother our mothers. When my turn comes for that, I hope I can heed my own advice, for even mothers sometimes need to be bathed, not only with water, but with love and understanding. And I can tell you, for sure, we will never outgrow our need for space to breathe.

My Boy's Life

Graham and I have a nightly ritual. After his bath, we sit in the rocking chair, away from the rest of the family, and make peace.

It is as necessary to us as waking, eating. This peace cleanses our battle-weary bodies of the daily frustrations of being the mother of a two-year-old and of being two. Our hugs, kisses, and nighttime stories help remind us both of the love we have as mother and son.

Daily we wage war against each other and those awful twos. He's angry because birds fly away when he wants to watch; the bag he fills overflows with blocks; he wants down when he's up, up when he's down. The whirlwind lasts much longer than I think I can stand.

I'm angry at him for not understanding how weary he makes me, angry at myself for not having more patience. He is just two.

Is he really the same child who, as a newborn, wrapped his tiny fingers around my own? He was instantly trusting then, giving me his love without thought of return. He knew little of his power over me then, but at two, he's learning. I feel guilty, for his love for me is still, always, unconditional; my anger toward him doesn't matter. I am unworthy of such remarkable love.

It's ironic, for our children need our unquestioning love most when loving them is hardest for us—this much I've learned in my short years as a mother. They need our reassurance: We do understand, it will be all right. If all we can offer them in these often-stormy years are laps to sit on, stories to share, and hugs at day's end, then we must always provide them.

So Graham and I make peace. When daylight comes again we have new ground for our battles, and as each day passes, our defenses weaken a little. Maybe in time, this peace will last.

MAMA'S BOY

I hear a clatter in the hall, and I can tell without looking up from my work that Meredith is playing dress-up again. Her feet click, scuff, click toward me, and I look to see what outrageous costume she's managed to put together this time. But I'm puzzled, for the Barbie bride-doll mask sits closer to the ground than usual, and those pink and blue heels clash sharply with the red corduroy pants above them.

"Mommy, pretty!" says Graham, holding in his hand a Barbie dressed in shimmering gold lamé. He's at it again. The last time I caught him undressing that doll (and trying to eat her shoes), I vowed to bone up on macho toys, maybe even buy him one of those He-man dolls everybody's talking about.

But from the looks of those blue eyes peeping at me from behind the mask, I may already be too late.

I'm open-minded. I know that today's child must be exposed to all kinds of toys. No gender stereotypes are we parents supposed to foster. I want Meredith to know how to pitch a ball, form a hypothesis as well as her brother, balance her checkbook as well as I can, debate, whatever it was boys were supposed to do better than girls when I was growing up.

But I don't worry about her. She is as at home with a hammer as she is with a tube of lipstick. Yet her list of career alternatives is typical of a five-year-old girl: babysitter, mall girl, cheerleader, ballerina. She only recently added writer to the list.

I've told her she that can do anything, that interest is half the battle.

But domineering women surround Graham at every turn. If not me, then it's Meredith and her cronies. No wonder he steals into her room as soon as the carpool picks her up, reappearing and reeking of perfume, a purse slung over his shoulder. The trucks, the basketball goal, his *Sesame Street* power tools go untouched in favor of Meredith's possessions.

My messages, though well meaning, are confusing. I don't fret when he plays with dolls (he'll be a better dad), or pretends to toss an omelet (his wife will appreciate my training him to cook).

But I do worry, that if I don't take drastic measures, his friends will, one day, label him "sissy," and all those other things mama's boys are known as. Yet I want him to maintain his gentle nature, his loving concern, already shown, for someone who's hurting.

So be tough, but gentle, I'll tell him. Learn to shoot a basketball (not a gun). Carry a handkerchief so you won't have to sneeze into your sleeve. Dig in the dirt, fight with your sister occasionally (in fun), but never forget your mother's birthday.

"GRRRRR!! POW!!" he screams, charging at me with the toy vacuum cleaner raised in defiance. But just when I think the crusade is working, he lapses into the familiar.

"I want pingernail," he says as I'm removing hot-pink polish from Meredith's nails. He holds his hand, ever so delicately, for me to see.

I bite my lip, thankful that just now there isn't time. "Maybe later," I say. Besides, hot pink is not his best color.

AND NOW WE ARE THREE

He is sleeping, his body a pretzel in his favorite chair. I don't dare smooth the wrinkles for fear of waking him. It's a rare midday break for me from a boy who now almost never sleeps anymore, and I'm grateful for the quiet.

Worn out from yesterday's birthday festivities, my sleeping three-year-old vaguely reminds me of the drowsy day-old newborn I nuzzled close in the hospital. That child was hard to wake, opening his eyes only to eat at first. Satisfied, he was off to sleep again, until his tummy called.

This child closes his eyes only when he has upturned every game, sofa cushion, and puzzle piece within reach. Today alone, he has camped out in his sleeping bag, brushed his teeth by the campfire, rescued a cowgirl (me) from laundry bandits with his new holster and guns, built and demolished log houses, constructed Tinker Toy trucks, eaten three meals. And it is barely noon.

They are one, the newborn and the toddler, though they seldom resemble each other except when Graham's eyes are closed, and he is sleeping.

The months between the two are a blur of diaper sizes, drowsy feedings, tiny training wheels, and *Ghostbusters*. And lots and lots of screaming.

Of course Year Two was the longest, most painful part of it, and the most memorable. We thought it would never end.

And now we are three.

I'm tired today, too, perhaps because I'm aware that, for the second time in this family, we've survived the twos with only a few scratches.

Last year we made peace with each other at the end of each day. Our nightly rocking mending fences broken by angry words and tears, fortified us so we didn't break them down quite so far the next day.

Now when we rock, we rarely think of mending each other's feelings. Though we still butt heads, my three-year-old throws one tantrum a day instead of a dozen, gives mounds of kisses when I'm most frustrated with him, and sings, all day long, the same three songs, so that even I wake up singing them.

I can only wonder what tomorrow will bring. Today I'll enjoy him sleeping. When he wakes, we'll likely share a couple of dozen games of baseball with his new glove while singing B-I-N-G-O at the top of our lungs.

But I'm grateful, since there is always room for a little more music.

PARTING IS SUCH SWEET SORROW

The new black backpack hangs on a peg in my son's room, filled with all he'll need for kindergarten: safety scissors, new Crayolas (sixteen-count), neon pencil box, Elmer's glue, and one shiny, new, unsharpened pencil.

He has packed and unpacked the treasures daily, eager to get to work at whatever he is imagining kindergartners do once the class door closes behind their anxious mothers.

I, on the other hand, am not so sure I'm ready for kindergarten. It's not what he'll do that troubles me, but what finding myself in an empty house for part of the day will do to me. My five-and-a-half-year-old, my baby, is packing his bags and going off to school, leaving me to pick up his Legos and myself as I send him on to a world foreign to both of us.

He is wondering where the bathroom is, when's snack time, and how long he'll have until it's time to go outside. I can't help wondering how he (and I) will be changed when he comes home this afternoon.

I know about kindergarten. I've been through this before. His sister, today an ancient third-grader, gathered her own kindergarten wares three years ago. In tears and trembling, the two of us entered the vast unknown of public school.

But as soon as she found her name on the top of one of the tables, its letters neatly formed and laminated for life, my daughter knew that school was indeed the place for her.

It was the magic of lamination that attracted her, I think, appealing to her sense of order, of new rules to be learned and followed. She'd grown tired of the ones at home. I wondered then if her life—like her name— could be perpetually preserved in laminate so she wouldn't grow up, grow away from me, any more than she already had at that moment. She simply started kindergarten, but I thought she'd left me forever.

Meredith never looked back. She didn't see me huddled against the back of the classroom door, my heart tearing into tiny pieces at having to let go of her hand.

But my consolation was the small boy who held the other one, toddling next to me down the hall. "We've got a long time yet," I remember thinking then. There would still be many hours for watching *Sesame Street* together, shoes to learn to tie, and hugs to give before he would leave me. It seemed like an endless field of early fall days for us to fill with whatever we liked, now that Big Sister had a life of her own.

Yet, suddenly, our long time together is just about over.

Surely I must be mistaken. The last time I looked, my baby son was crawling around in OshKosh overalls and tennis shoes without a single scrape on the toes.

The baby I remember hardly resembles the boy who leaves me today. In well-worn Nikes, black Umbros, and a new "Leopard" mascot T-shirt, he jumps high, dribbles a ball between his legs, trades baseball cards with his friends, and kicks his sister when he gets the notion. Graham's once-new baby blanket is a web of yellow yarn, and I'm always finding pieces of it in corners all over the house.

As I prepare myself for leaving him today by his own carefully laminated name, I know that this time there will be nobody to hold my hand as I weep in the kindergarten hall.

But come to think of it, if I'm honest, perhaps the tears won't come so freely today as they did for my daughter. This second letting go will be far different from the first. I've been losing Graham in little bits and pieces ever since he took his first steps away from me at nine months old. And I most recently noticed it when a friend caught him riding his bike around the block, without his helmet and without permission. I suppose it's just this way with mothers and sons. You kiss them on the head, shaking your own and hoping they'll show up in a while to kiss you back.

At least I can be pretty sure this time where Graham's going. And it's a relief, frankly, to know that I'll find a few corners of quiet in the house once he's firmly settled at his new teacher's feet. We haven't known quiet around here in a very long time.

For five-and-a-half, my sweet kindergartner is a whirling dervish, seldom taking time to stop, look, and listen for any reason anymore. He talks incessantly at mealtime, whines when he doesn't get his way. And daily we're barraged with bathroom words set to his five-year-old idea of rap music. He ambushes me on my way to the laundry with an arsenal of make-believe weapons.

I feel a little guilty about my selfish thoughts, so I seek counsel from my neighbor, who sent her only son to kindergarten a couple of years ago. Expecting her to tell me I'd regret my feelings, I was caught by her answer.

"My son's first day of school was the happiest day of my life," she told me. "I couldn't wait for school to start."

And so our new life apart from each other begins. But before I leave Graham in his new classroom amid twenty-five or so smiling faces, I'll help him find the bathroom. I'll remind him to pay attention, to mind his manners, and to keep his hands to himself. And I won't forget to kiss his forehead.

I doubt, somehow, that I'll be alone in the hall once the door is closed. My neighbor will probably be there, waiting to sneak in a high-five.

And maybe if I'm lucky, I'll only have to wait for the bus to drop off its weary traveler this afternoon to get my kiss back.

UNDER COVER

I've been cleaning Graham's room, which, for the mother of an eight-year-old boy, requires perseverance, rubber gloves, and hip boots. I put this task off as long as possible—weeks have passed since the last time—his clothes now groping the outside of the dresser, books scattered in makeshift skyscrapers on the floor, every speck of everything, even dust, out of place. Though I require him to clean his own room, at least on Saturdays, when he walks in after my day's cleaning, posters fall from the walls, and crayons drip wax from their tips, all by themselves, onto the carpet.

And there is the food. During past cleanup expeditions I may have unwittingly thrown out a cure for cancer disguised as purple fungus on an unidentifiable food item stashed in a toy drawer. Pretzels have been stuffed under mounds of toy bears, empty Fruit Rollup boxes have been scattered under the bed, and even some Puppy Chow has been stored in a small plastic box that usually houses a video game. Don't ask me why. He is like a squirrel, saving up for who knows what, perhaps for those days when he finds the pantry bare. He doesn't yet realize that its emptiness means the contents have defied gravity and moved upstairs to his room. Of course, when questioned, he's totally innocent of any crime.

I'm positive this is a trait of the male species, for across the hall, Meredith's room is "just so," every CD and book in place, nary a food crumb in sight, since House Rule Number 32 is "don't eat anywhere except the kitchen." She probably just hides it better than her brother.

Today I tread lightly through his muddle, wary of what I may find. The Legos have been building by themselves in the middle of the room for days now, and I don't dare disturb them for fear I'll destroy some intergalactic module embarking on a secret mission to steal Oreos from the kitchen.

I should be glad that misplacing food is usually Graham's only overt violation. Soon enough, I'm sure, I'll find age-inappropriate magazines, instead of potato chips, stuffed between mattress and box spring.

On another day, he'd be quick to halt my investigations, but he left today on a weekend trip with Dad. I am wild with anticipation, imagining my two days to rake the mess into a huge pile for the garbage man.

I change the sheets, lifting the bedcovers from the floor where he left them piled this morning, but to my surprise, no plastic soldiers fall from their hiding places, no Lego men are left without their camouflage. At the foot of the pile is a small yellow patch of yarn and fur I was sure he'd taken with him; he wouldn't go away two entire days without his blanket, or his constant night companion, dear Chick. Would he?

The blanket isn't really a blanket anymore. A web is a more apt description for the shreds of string that I once wrapped him in at night. It was love at first feel between this blanket and my boy. On his first day home, he slept quietly in the baby seat at my feet, nudging the corners of his new blanket with his nose. No ordinary cover, it has been a fort when hung with rubber bands between doorknobs, given the wearer super powers when worn as a cape, and kept us from discovering him hidden within our sight. It calmed him when fatigue became too much to bear, many times when I had no luck myself. Some nights now, Graham covers his entire head with it as he tumbles off to sleep. He loved every piece of silken edging away from this blanket years ago. Chick, Blanket's cohort, was an Easter Bunny afterthought whose arms and legs have seen a stitch or two.

So how could Graham leave these comrades abandoned on the floor of his room like old socks that have grown too small? In trips past, the two are usually last in, first out of the suitcase, a small piece of home for my homebody son. But this time, I can only assume that leaving them behind has something to do with my son's beginning to grow from the young boy into the older one. Taking his blanket along on an outing with the guys wouldn't be cool.

Blankets and stuffed toys just don't mix with baseball gloves and fishing reels, though I'm sure Chick and Blanket are wondering why they were left behind for this very first time. The time has finally come when Dad's company supercedes the need for any other, and while I'm glad for both father and son, I am a bit sad, too. Soon, these forgotten particles of childhood will be tossed from the bed into a box earmarked for the attic, though I can't bear that thought just now; I'd counted on packing them up for the dorm room in another ten years; if I couldn't be there, at least my co-comforters would. But by then, the blanket will be a single strand. Who knows what will have become of Chick.

I fold the blanket as neatly as its form will hold and place it under Chick, who props against the pillow, waiting patiently for his friend's return. Somehow cleaning has lost its urgency, and I head back to the kitchen to ponder my discovery. Later on, when the phone rings, I am almost relieved to learn that Graham has a fever, and the boys are headed home early from their outing.

Under cover of night he comes in curled on my husband's shoulder, and as we slip him into bed, he sleepily spies his forgotten companions. The boy's arm grips Chick's neck, tucks the blanket quickly underneath his chin, and in seconds he is sleeping. Watching him, I vow to hand-wash the blanket from now on, not wanting to lose another piece of it. Looks like I won't need to go to the attic, either, in search of that empty box just yet.

HEADED FOR THE WILD THINGS

Graham is reading, and from the door I can see that his choice of books this night won't likely be turned in for credit. It's a tattered paperback, *Where the Wild Things Are*, one of his favorites when he was little.

"'And when he came to the place where the wild things are,'" I recite, "'they ROARED their terrible roars, GNASHED their terrible teeth and ROLLED their terrible eyes....'" But I fumble with the rest.

How could I have forgotten a single line of this story, burnished into my brain from reading it night after night when he was small?

"'Till Max said "BE STILL!"'" Graham bellows, and I'm able to finish... "'And tamed them with the magic trick of staring into all their yellow eyes without blinking once.'"

Reading the story together all those years ago stilled him, my little wild thing. It fostered our reconnection each night after days filled with too many "nos." I'd rock him, clean and warm in his footed pajamas, and he'd mouth the words around his pacifier as I read.

But why would he pull out this old story now, its cover long gone, the pages scribbled on in purple crayon? He is fourteen, after all.

Could be he's searching for clues. He's headed to where the real wild things are soon—high school—and maybe he wants to remember how to tame them. Earlier in the week, we ventured into the catacombs of the high school he'll be attending in the fall. Watching him lumber through the halls next to his friends, it was easy to forget that he is still that boy who loved the courageous Max and his wild friends. Towering over the others, my child stands six feet in his socks, his buddies flanking him like sprouts. All angles and lines, he's useful when I need help pulling things down from tall cabinets or putting them back, but I know he sometimes feels ungainly. Standing in shoes my father's size, he is truly a man-child, wavering and a little unsure of which way to go.

I don't remember liking very much about fourteen-year-old boys when I was his age. I was a bundle of emotion, uncomfortable in my own skin. The boys I knew were constantly talking about sports and cars, caring very little about girls as far as I knew.

Boys that age haven't changed much, but I've found myself enjoying Graham and his friends, an eclectic group that complements his sardonic sense of humor. Graham's world is tennis and Scouts, guitar and big-wheeled trucks, school (which he lovingly hates) and dances, where swarms of giggling girls whirl around him and his buddies, all of whom care more about the music than about their present company, though he does have a few Anna Kournikova posters hanging around.

He is teaching himself to play the guitar, downloading tablature from his favorite musicians. One night, strumming and crooning, he sat behind my office chair to serenade me. Usually it's "Stairway to Heaven," but on this night he bellowed "House of the Rising Sun," a song about another boy and other wild things, a song common to both our generations. Since no one else was in the house to tell me not to, I crooned too, our voices blending in a surprising harmony.

There is no better moment than this, I thought, a boy who will still sing with his mother, play for her when she needs it most. I long to keep him just this way, the child who can love Max and Led Zeppelin at the same time.

But I know his emerging passion for whatever comes next will soon take over. Like all of us, he's ready to see what it's like to be a little less like Max and a little more like his yellow-eyed monster friends.

So as we move through this next stage, I'll leave the light burning and keep the porridge hot, waiting to see just who he'll finally be.

JUST THE RIGHT MUSIC

There was always music coming from somewhere inside my son. The laughing baby, the talkative toddler, the foot clap-clap on the kitchen floor—all music to me when he was growing.

Now, at fifteen, Graham continues the theme, strumming along with the stereo on one of his two guitars. He's moved from notes to noise to real music, spends hours playing, and is even in a band.

I don't share his talent. A mediocre piano student, I played once for Sunday school when I was in fourth grade, but after hitting a sour note in the fifth bar, I froze. To this day I can't hear "In the Cross of Christ I Glory," key of C, without reliving that F-sharp.

But we try to correct our childhood shortcomings through our offspring. Piano lessons for both my kids would do it.

My daughter caught on quickly. I added my son to the mix, multiplying my pride. Or so I thought.

It was his second recital, I think. The song called for him to take his hands from the keys and clap. Though he was following the music, the clapping seemed bizarre. He was mortified. I cringed. He quit after that song, refusing ever to set bottom on a piano bench again.

In the years that followed, Graham tried other things. There was a short basketball season, during which he scored only one basket. There was baseball, which he played but didn't love. He took up swimming, too, but was embarrassed by the suits.

Then, one day, he tried the guitar.

Did I mention I took guitar, too? I tried my hand on a Yamaha acoustic, strung left-handed, like me. I sat on a hard plastic chair at the Baptist church alongside a boy my age whose guitar was already a piece of himself, a boy who would grow up to play in a band and produce gospel music.

I kept trying to find my gift. I took a sewing class, studying the logic of a Butterick pattern and of words like "interfacing," eventually sewing a flowered shift that never quite fit. My best friend, in the same class, transformed her piece of hot-pink shantung into a statement. Years later she would move to New York, design clothes, and become a highly successful fashion consultant whose favorite color is still hot pink.

Though I couldn't play music, I loved listening and would bend my ear closely to Jim Croce on the eight-track, listening to every single pluck of the strings. But it was the words he strung together that captured my soul. That's when I first began to realize that words—not music, not sewing—were my passion.

When Graham asked for guitar lessons, I was skeptical. But we dragged out the old Yamaha and had it restrung. He taught himself. Night after night I found him, guitar in his lap, plucking it out. In no time he was playing chords. We bought him a new, steel-stringed instrument, and soon he was strumming through the house like a troubadour.

As I listen to the rock of his electric guitar roll through the house, I can't imagine that I once thought he was as musically inept as I am. When he gathers with his friends to jam, or with Scott, his guitar teacher, who would rather jam than eat and is teaching my son the same, I know he's found that thing that moves him. It is there, inside this sometimes timid young man, in his soul when his fingers touch the strings.

And now, the boy I raised plays the intro to Jim Croce's "Time in a Bottle" for me, carefully plucking the notes with his angular fingers, calling me in to hear it only when he has gotten it right. Shy about it still, he doesn't sing the words, yet I understand how this piece of wood and wire has captured that important piece of him and will probably never let go. No clapping required. Only applause.

Nobody's Shadow

PERFECT FIT

We've been searching for the perfect shoes, my daughter and I, for yet another milestone—fifth-grade graduation. We meander from one mall store to the next requesting the elusive size-eight quad that, if found, would fit both Meredith's foot and mine. I try to direct her to a dress flat I like, in a color I need, so we could share. But she will have her own shoes, thank you.

Don't say one more time how expensive shoes are in her size, because it's all my fault that her feet are hard to fit anyway. She doesn't know that once in the past week I was forced to borrow her white Keds because mine were in the wash. A perfect fit, mind you, but her shoes, not mine.

She hobbles across the department store floor in narrow dress shoes that flip off of her heel. Too wide again, so our search resumes. I wonder how much capital it would take to open my own shoe store for pre-teens who don't want to wear styles their mothers choose. Surely, I would make enough to buy shoes for both of us that truly fit.

How can it be that we are wearing the same size? Shouldn't mothers forever be a size larger than daughters, a step ahead on the sidewalk, making sure the street's safe to cross?

Used to be that shoe buying meant a children's shoe store and a nice pair of Mary Janes. I was the only family member cursed to return home with arms empty from a whole day's shoe searching. Now, though, I envision the years ahead as we shop in vain together, scouring the Southeast for anything in our size. I take no pleasure in Meredith's company, wishing she'd inherited the Rountree B-width, instead of mine. It has been struggle enough for me alone.

Today shoe shopping reduces the two of us to tears; Meredith cries from frustration at pulling her sneakers off and on, trying to keep the foot stocking on, searching for women's shoes when she wants kid shoes, only bigger. She doesn't care that I know how she feels, longing only to find something, anything, to fit so she won't be caught wearing my shoes on the graduation stage in front of all of her friends.

My tears, though, come not from our fruitless shoe search, but from knowing, as we edge toward her last day of elementary school, we are at yet another turn, one I've taken far too many times already. The twinge is familiar, unwelcome and always surprising, first noticed in the excitement of a new tooth, again when she tied her own shoes, when she walked alone into preschool, and dozens of other times in the last dozen years. Today I feel it as my child grows to look me in the eye, to wear my shoes long after she has stopped playing dress-up. This will fade soon, but I dread its return, for in time it will mean other graduations, other turns my daughter will make alone.

Looking at her now, her lean fingers touching the toes of shoes lined up like parade marchers on the store shelves, I think back to a moment ago when I slipped a tiny lace bootie onto toes shaped remarkably like mine. Since then, she has had her own parade of favorites: pink Kmart slip-ons, black-patent "clap" shoes, Keds. Now she leans toward Sambas and woven sandals, rolling her eyes at my more practical suggestions. Her feet, it seems, are always changing, growing into yet another size, many times larger than I ever dreamed she'd wear the first time I smoothed her tiny toes with my fingers.

I am obsessing again, but knowing the shoes we search for will take her into yet one more new stage gives me just cause. I looked away from lace booties, only to turn my head back and find her growing within inches of me, playing the piano, having a boy friend, making cookies when I've long since lost the time. Not long ago, I was there in those same shoes, an eleven-year-old twirling my size eights in front of my own mother. Blink. Here stands my child.

Could it be that Meredith was so busy growing in and out of shoes that I never even noticed the change until now?

Soon enough she'll be buying her own shoes, standing on that awkward measure without me to press down on her toe. I worry that she'll forget to tell the salesman about her narrow heel, that she'll have trouble finding shoes to fit—life to fit—without me there beside her, directing the show.

Our lives have been connected like so many threads woven into our family cloth. But over time, she has pulled a few threads out to make her own cloth, taking some from me, some from friends, teachers and others who have no connection to me except through my child.

Soon she'll pass me by as she slips from elementary school to middle school and beyond. I hope she'll find this next transition as simple as slipping from shoe one size to the next, but it won't be so easy for me. I doubt that changes brought about by my growing children will ever stop.

This afternoon the elementary-school bell will ring for the last time for Meredith, and when she rushes into the house, spilling her shoes and her excitement onto the floor, I'll be there to pick up her old shoes, wherever she leaves them. Though they may one day be a bit too tight in the toes for her, I take comfort in knowing these particular shoes will always fit me.

POETIC LICENSE

My refrigerator door is a composite of family treasures. One corner holds a yellowing comic about mothers and a teasing shot of my seventy-one-year-old father sporting a grandson's knock-off Oakley sunglasses. Magnets advertising everything from pizza delivery and our favorite restaurant in France to the plumber and the veterinarian hold fast reminders of appointments to be kept or changed.

But the spot above the ice-and-water dispenser is my treasure, because it hosts a set of magnetic words swirling with crazy messages left by friends and family. This is everyman's corner, luring even the most reluctant kitchen poet to deposit a thought in exchange for food and drink.

I have my favorites among these sayings, which are scrambled as easily as Scrabble letters. I survey them often, choosing the best ones to record for keeps. "Soar on a pound puppy" was the very first, left by a funny friend.

"Wax hair will not do"—author unknown—but someone, no doubt, who brushed up against my son after his gelled hair had dried to a stiff peak. There's an ode to our recently departed grandmother: "As Honey sings to you, picture a bittersweet symphony," mixed with hopeful messages from me—"the cook wants diamonds"—in case my husband needs something to read when he is scavenging. Maybe I should choose my words more carefully, since just yesterday I discovered a scramble that turned my wish list around: "Pound the cook."

Though most of these magnetic messages are harmless, sometimes words converge that strike me right to the quick: "Mothers cry frantically when their shadows drive."

My sixteen-year-old daughter, Meredith, left that one, and I get the joke. She's been talking in metaphors since she was three, when she first noticed the broken moon one morning on a trip to the store and asked me to find the missing piece. I cried then, thinking I was raising another writer, a real shadow for me to mentor.

But my firstborn—never a shadow to anyone—had other ideas: mall girl, office worker, interior designer, wedding planner. Though I vaguely remember her once or twice hiding behind my skirts, she soon learned that she could step outside the shadow her mother drew on the world and make her own.

Mothers cry frantically when their shadows drive.

There are days, of course, when the lines separating our shadows blur into one, but these are fewer now that she has a license to leave me. We seem to merge and separate often, like the yellow lines painted on the road she now drives all by herself.

"Where is the best place to get binders?" she asked just three days into sixteen. For a moment I forgot, trying to think of an hour to peel away from my work to take her. A natural mistake, when your shadow has been sewn to your feet for so long.

"How do you get there?" she asked next. I pictured her behind the wheel of her used Volvo, driving down a congested street near our house. Without me, how would she know not to run that new red light? What if she got lost? Or hurt?

I pretended to be nonplussed, describing the safest route there and home, but picturing her in my mind being run down by oncoming traffic. Could she accurately judge distances between cars? What if the engine stalled in the middle of her turn?

I heard the keys jingle, and she was off, the merging over until another time.

There have been hundreds of these shadow dances through the years, but this birthday may have marked the hardest yet. We were all up early, her dad riding with her to the driver's license office at 8:00 a.m., and within a half-hour, the phone was ringing, her voice singing to me of her new independence. I hung up, scrambling eggs and taking solace in the fact that she was getting a city street map for her birthday—a small piece of me to take with her on the road.

But this is the child who, when asked "What is the one thing you'd take with you if you were stranded on a desert island?," said "tour guide" without a thought. No compass, no water or rations, just a tawny guide to show her the way. Who needs Mom when you can have that?

She spent her Big Day not once looking back, except, thankfully, when backing out of the driveway. While she was gone, I combed the cabinet for pictures of her when she was small.

I thought I was prepared. In the last few months, half a dozen new drivers have shown up at our house, circling our block like veterans, and though one or two have backed over the grass, the mailbox, remarkably, still stands guard at the curb. These are the same kids who played dress-up in my bridesmaid's dresses, burned cookies in my kitchen, and giggled about boys late into the night. And they're driving?

I can't be old enough for this. I still recall clearly the day I got my own license, my mother driving me downtown in my homemade miniskirt. I learned to drive on narrow country roads, and I'm sure I was at least eighteen before I drove on an Interstate. But my child drove down I-95 six months ago. She's learned to merge into traffic and finagle a parking place at the mall, with me directing, of course, until now.

What she needs, I'm convinced, is the bumper sticker that says, "Don't like my driving? Call my mom." When I say as much, I only get eye rolling and sighs, a look that says I've long forgotten how good it feels to finally step out of the family minivan and shine your own headlights.

A couple of days after her birthday, Meredith took me outside to show how she'd made her solid hand-me-down vehicle her own—the air-freshener she'd hidden next to the seat, the packs of gum in the glove compartment, the emergency kit we gave her for her birthday, all neatly stored in case of need. With Tim McGraw blaring on the radio, she zips off to Kmart for pencils, to a friend's house, and to her favorite hamburger joint to meet her friends—all of whom have driven themselves there because they can. While they chat and chow down on burgers and shakes, their mothers are all back at home, like me, biting instead into their nails.

"I just love to drive," she says to me, home safely, this time, from school. "It makes going to school worth it, knowing I get to drive home."

Within minutes I notice she's looking around for her brother, and I feel another trip is in the offing. This time it's for gas; seems she'd never really paid attention the hundreds of times I'd gotten it for myself. I guess it's an acceptable use for a younger brother, since he's been pumping my gas for a couple of years now. And because he is still somewhat in my shadow, I feel like she's taking a little piece of me along.

I watch Meredith's comings and goings, and I can't help recalling the favorite "Shadow" poem by Robert Louis Stevenson I used to read to her when she was small. Yes, I had a little shadow once who was very much like me from the heels up to the head. I always thought she'd be with me, but somewhere along the way, she got a taste of the sunshine and switched places with me when I wasn't looking.

Mothers cry frantically when their shadows drive.

SHATTERED

It's 11:45 p.m., and I check the clock, wondering where my child is. First night out of school, of being a "senior." She's checked in three times, but I still worry. She should be home in fifteen minutes.

Through the open window I hear her car, the door slam, the garage door moan, lights clicking off as she makes her way upstairs. Another night, home safe again. I breathe.

"Mom," she says, peeking in. "There was a really bad wreck tonight. Kids from Leesville High School have been killed. I'm going upstairs to see if I can find anything out."

My heart skips. We'd watched an old home video, back when we knew where our kids were every minute. We hadn't heard. I lie in the dark, think of four houses somewhere nearby, click off the names of kids I know who go to Leesville, pray for them. Pray for the four families who I know won't ever sleep again, ever breathe, after this night.

I thank God that my own child is home, on the phone with her friends, even though it's way past the time that we allow it. It is the night before graduation. Sad enough to *feel* you are losing your friends. A different story to *know* they're lost.

At daybreak I rise and turn on the news. Three from Leesville killed, and one from my daughter's high school. I stand in front of the television, wondering if she knows this boy, thinking she probably does not.

Ice cream. The paper says they were going for ice cream. Goodberrys. Just down the street. Good kids all. Whenever are they not?

7:30 a.m. My friend Grace calls and the boy, Mike, was indeed a friend. Of both our daughters. I long to find his picture in the yearbook, but I'd have to wake Meredith to find it, and I'm not ready to do that. What will I say?

8:15 a.m. The phone rings again. Nick, my daughter's friend forever; I have to wake her now. I do, and she cries—can't remember Nick's phone number. She's out the door in fifteen minutes, headed to Nick's, but who knows where she'll end up? Perhaps with her friends who will spend the day recalling when they last saw Mike. She calls to say they are headed to the accident site.

Don't our children know that we worry about this very thing every single time they walk out the door? Every time they say "I'm going to so-and-so's house; I'm going to Bojangles, to Goodberrys, I'm going, going…," and we say, "Fine," but pray it doesn't mean "gone," and our hearts stop, never to really start again until we see them. Don't they know?

I see her again at Sanderson, her small clutch of friends not knowing what to do or say, just wanting to be together. A reporter loiters close by.

Flowers begin to show up in the memorial garden. A small card that says simply "For Mike" brings me to tears. I didn't know this boy, but can remember him on my doorstep one afternoon late last summer; my heart chokes for his mother. My child studied for exams with him just last week.

At home my son says he played tennis last summer with Brian, the brother of one of his friends. I try to recall him and can remember his little sister well. I think of her life now.

I think of other mothers I know of who have lost children. Rocky Mountain spotted fever. Leukemia. An accidental stabbing. The fire in Chapel Hill. And wrecks, always wrecks. It is the one communal worry we share but don't speak of, the one thing we can't protect our children from, not ever.

Don't they know? Our children who are so quick to grab the keys and head out for ice cream. Don't they know that we don't really sleep, breathe? That we never will, if they don't come home?

Later, I hug my son more than he wants me to, say " Be careful …," cry a little, even though he is only crossing the street.

The Importance of Being a Coed

Our high-school senior-to-be snips when Dad can't find the right parking lot, while I try not to think about where we're going. We bundle ourselves against the drizzle, and head toward this, our first college visit, taking our seats in the auditorium. I scan the day's agenda, and my throat tightens when I see that my daughter will attend a college class without me.

"This seems a little surreal," Dad whispers. "I still dream about not getting to class on time."

"Not one cute boy here," the coed-to-be observes, surveying the crowd. How could I forget the real reason for college planning?

We're just beginning the college search for our headstrong seventeen-year-old. We've studied *U.S. News & World Report,* shopped online for offerings in interior design, photography, and communications, though she is not sure she's interested in those, you understand. Our discussions often end in frustration—fear really. None of us is sure of what's ahead. Twenty-five years ago I chose where I wanted to go and went. Simple as that. Today finding an alma mater requires consultants in everything from SAT prep to dormitory décor.

Each week our mailbox ripens with slick brochures featuring fresh-faced coeds, facing down computers, scowling behind television cameras, smiling as they walk to class. Study abroad, internships, fellowships—the copy lures like a Madison Avenue sales pitch, though I don't think our child has read a single word.

This day's recruitment video features even more fresh-faced kids talking about college life, how they were *transformed* by choosing this particular place.

I remember dreaming I'd be transformed, too, far from the cinderblock building that was my high school home, and my child's face reveals her own optimism. It's easy to forget the realities of acceptance—grades, SAT scores, costs—when a stranger claims to believe in your endless potential.

The video ends, of course, with music. Who couldn't use John Williams to score the backdrop for her dreams? My throat fills again; then tears drip, just a few. My child's sidelong glance tells all.

Our tour guide is nice, but not cute. He walks us through the frigid mist to the state-of-the-art activity center—workout rooms, gyms, a pool, where through glass walls, we see students and professors in motion. I marvel at this opportunity to fend off the freshman fifteen. Though we had no set-up like this in college, it's family folklore that my only college exercise was walking to the Krispy Kreme and back.

"One," the daughter says. "I see one. When I count like that, you'll know that's how many cute guys I've seen."

At the communications school the fully stocked Macintosh lab and the TV studio run by students sit almost empty today.

"Zero," I hear from behind me.

We cross the quad—is there a college without one?—where oak branches scratch the cold gray sky. "Everybody comes here when the weather is warm," the guide says, but it's hard to picture. Only ice-bitten tourists are out today.

In the library, at last, students, most huddled in front of computers—instant-messaging their friends?

"Three," she says. "Maybe four. And there are way too many cute girls."

Finally, they allow us in from the cold to the cafeteria, a food court really. Salad bars, pasta stations, fried zucchini, hot soup, no mystery meat that I can see.

After lunch, we part ways. I watch, throat clogged, as she follows the line upstairs, and we take our seats again to be counseled on how to fund the bottom line.

"That was the strangest class I've ever been to," she says at day's end. "The teacher talked about how it was our job to change the world." Strange, indeed. And exciting.

I've heard stories about families who take a child to college, then gather in her room and cry for an hour, fingering trinkets left behind. That will be me, my daily activity; my daughter's already said as much. Just the fact of her leaving, and not even soon, is changing my world—much like her arrival in it. I have over a year to prepare, but there is so much trinket fingering to do.

A CASE OF SENIORITIS

I live with two teenagers, so there is always somebody out of sorts at my house. Lately it's Big Sister. She's stricken with senioritis, the so-called malaise that creeps over the oldest high-school students as they wait for real life to begin. Meredith routinely announces she's ready to pack her bags and move to college. Today is not soon enough.

She's tired of constantly pushing herself, competing with friends who seem to make stellar grades with ease. Advanced-placement and honors courses, student government responsibilities, her job on the school newspaper—all more than she can handle at times, so she longs for escape.

It's leaving all she used to cherish that seems most important to her now. She can't wait to share a room for the first time in her life and live in a dorm with no private bath, filled with other teenagers she has yet to meet. She already knows she prefers their company over her family's.

The high-school counselors have told us that this is the first step toward independence for our seniors, that they are ripping those ties they've had to us by rejecting most about their lives now, focusing more on what they dream of being.

The rest of us waltz precariously around Meredith as she comes and goes. I never know just how far she'll go or when she'll ricochet back to me.

I'm not too far removed from high school to recall that longing for anything and everything new. I was tired of looking at the same old faces I'd known since kindergarten, faces with no surprises left in them. When the college catalogues arrived at my house so full of ideas I'd never dreamed of, I finally understood how much life there was outside my little town, and I couldn't wait to live it.

There are so many things I wish to tell her now, if only she would listen. I want to tell her that this is the first of many times she'll long for change, and that most often it's worth the wait. That in not too many years, she'll be wishing she could see those same old faces she knew by heart in high school, that she'll treasure most of all the friends who knew her before she knew herself. Leaving surely teaches you that. But she doesn't want to hear all this from me. I'm part of all that's old about her life.

My friends who've passed this stage tell me that seniors in high school are by nature cranky, at least in the first semester. We need them to be this way so we'll be glad when they move out. I can't imagine feeling that way about her, but I might.

Together now we wait for the mail, knowing all too well that her future rests in the hands of strangers who'll decide her course based on what they read about her on a few sheets of paper. That's pretty scary for both of us. She is so much more than the collection of minutiae she's been asked about herself. But right now, after all her hard work, she doesn't believe it.

The waiting feels a lot like those nine months I waited for her to be born, knowing something big was going to happen, but not at all sure what. At least then I had a little control over the outcome. With this I have none. I want to plop myself down in those admissions offices and dare them not to take her.

Not because I want her gone, but because they'll be so lucky to get her. If there is any doubt, all they need to do is ask me.

The Year of "We"

Let me say right off the bat that I think I've held myself together pretty well. Mothers of earlier high-school graduates advised me to keep the Kleenex handy all year because, even for the crusted, Senior Year is emotional.

I can vouch for that. We—and I mean the graduate, her parents, and her brother—have been through every piece of it together. Though

Meredith has been quite vocal about it being *her* year, *her* experience, she's taken the rest of us along for a very bumpy ride.

We've made it through college applications, grades that weren't quite what we'd hoped (and many that were), college acceptances (and rejections), prom, even Spring Break, each phase weaving its own emotional trauma into our family fabric. Elation, confusion, anger, sadness, worry, fear, disillusionment, and finally, anticipation. The last few weeks especially have been a tapestry of them all. Projects, computer crashes, farewell assemblies, scholarship notifications, parties, and we still have a few days yet to go.

Sure, I've shed some tears. Meredith sparkled, though my eyes welled when I read the graduation announcement, as she smoothed the mortarboard over her hair that first time, and now whenever I go into her room just to look at her. But we've laughed, too, as she downloaded "Pomp and Circumstance," and watched her leap around the room to the music, all blue polyester and bare feet.

We. It's always been the four of us, and though we've rehearsed for when she leaves for college, the reality of an entire Senior Year stood between us and the actual performance.

Yet, suddenly, it's over, this year of "we." In these days before graduation, "we" have faded into "she" and "the rest of us."

Maybe it was seeing her walk into the auditorium for Senior Assembly or watching her float down the aisle at church for Senior Sunday along with friends she's known since kindergarten.

Or maybe it was her goodbye message as editor of the school newspaper. She's never been good at goodbyes, except when leaving home. But she was eloquent, though even then I held myself together, tears only lightly dripping from my eyes.

I've kept telling myself—as I've heard a thousand times from other parents—it's time for her to go. Those "I'm-eighteen-and-I'm-an-adult!" tirades, the "Why-did-you-forget-to-do-this-or-that-for-me?" insinuations, the days when she thought she should be the focus of the whole family's attention—I won't miss any of that.

But then her math teacher had to ask me what I had done to raise such a remarkable young woman. Instantly my face was a dripping mop, my heart a whirl of tiny pieces reaching for wholeness again. Just like that, our "we" had broken apart.

What *did* I do? I wish I could remember every single detail, every good choice I made as her mother, so I could tell her when she becomes a mother to do the same thing. To raise a daughter just like she is.

When she was small, I took full credit for all the things she did that made me proud and the things that didn't. Now my once-bow-haired child is remarkable in someone else's eyes for being exactly what I'd hoped she'd be: strong, independent, creative, capable, and kind. And the credit is solely hers. Meredith is who she is despite the good choices I made and the thousands of times I fell short. Thank goodness my mistakes didn't stick.

Is there not a child who is remarkable just because she is yours? Just because she looks back at you on that very first day of life with her dancing eyes open wide to your face and wondering? Just because moments later, she bounces to the tune of "Pomp and Circumstance," all blue polyester and bare feet, looking away from you and at her new world ahead with those same dancing eyes? Because of the millions of moments in between, now and to come, just because, because?

But You Just Got Here

What they don't tell you about babies is that they leave. Right from the minute they're born, they are leaving you. You're ready, of course, because your toes are swollen, their knees are crowding your rib cage, and you say if only they would go ahead and come out. And then they do, and you say, "Oh, I didn't realize . . .."

Didn't realize that soon enough they'll learn to walk without holding your hand, put on a shirt by themselves even if it's the wrong color, draw out their ABCs in large blocks. Later they'll learn algebra, which you could never do, and spell words like plethora, which you can. And while they're learning all these things, they're looking into your eyes, saying, "I will never leave you," and they are lying. And you don't realize when you look back and say, "Don't ever leave," you're lying, too.

Of course you want them to—grow up, that is—and do all those things you've been doing for them, so they'll be independent, responsible, whatever. It says so much about you, really. But this is a bittersweet moment if there ever was one, wanting them to grow up, wishing they wouldn't, knowing they will.

My daughter leaves this week for college. The guest room is filled with new towels and sheets, a new laundry basket, a sewing kit she'll likely never use, pencils and paper, laptop and printer, a lamp decorated to match her comforter, even some Neosporin, just in case. We've sorted through and shifted in the past few weeks, making room for this new place in her life. In both our lives. She can't wait.

I know the feeling. In the weeks before I left for college, my mother and I combed the aisles at Towel Town for a laundry basket (which I still have) and yellow and green towels and sheets for me to take with me. What freedom to have linens I didn't have to share with anyone, a laundry basket filled only with my things.

The day I left, my mother stood at the kitchen sink with her back to me and cried. She is not a crier, but the next day would be my eighteenth birthday, and she couldn't bake me a cake. I didn't know then that her tears were for all the cakes to come. I wasn't thinking about her because for the first time in my life I was eager to leave, ready to make my own birthday cakes. If only I'd known how much I'd miss hers.

That night, at the stroke of midnight, I swilled my first legal beer, surrounded by friends I'd met who would become lifelong. The band at Charlie Goodnight's sang "Happy Birthday" to me. "If this is college," I thought, "I've come to the right place."

I've never been very good at leaving, no matter what's on the other side. My one stint at a two-week summer camp ended in three days. And when I was newly married and living far from home, I would sob for miles after every visit as we drove away, thinking I'd never see home again, the way it was. Those same feelings have hit me again and again these last few weeks. Sometimes there is little difference between leaving and being left.

It seems more than coincidental, Meredith points out, that when we part ways in her newly outfitted dorm room Saturday, it will be the day before my birthday, just as it was twenty-seven years ago when my mother left me in mine.

Meredith won't be thinking about me. She'll be meeting new friends who will become lifelong, and I'm certain she'll be headed for the band.

Maybe she'll ask them to sing for my birthday. And maybe my mother will remember how I'm feeling and finally bake me that cake.

Mother Me

When I heard the news of the death of the beloved Fred Rogers, just as this book was going to press in February 2003, my mother friends and I spent a teary afternoon remembering all he had given us and our children. It was as if we'd lost a favorite uncle whose passing meant the world was not quite as nice a place as it was when he was around. I wrote this letter in 1989 but never mailed it. Now, more than ever, I wish I had.

Dear Mr. Rogers:

How is it that you greet my children with such patience and love, just when mine has run out? Don't you know that it's five o'clock, and my wild-creature children are on the prowl?

I doubt you care what time it is, for your musical welcome lovingly lures them into closed-captioned captivity, setting me free, for the moment, from a day filled with frustration.

I can only guess the number of times I've put on shoes and socks today (my own just once). Or changed soggy underwear, wiped bottoms and tears, cornered and cajoled to brush teeth, to eat without standing in the chair or burping at the table.

Don't swing on my office door, or it will fall; it did. Don't climb on the arms of that chair, or you'll get hurt. He did.

Time-outs too many to count, as are the times the laundry has been washed and folded and used again. So many angry words fill my head that I am literally shaking. We tried to hug the anger away, and it only worked a little.

But there you are, opening your door, soothing them with your staccato piano notes just like my father used to play, slowing them down, stilling them for a few short minutes, so I can be still myself. Nobody can get hurt from just sitting, and I know you'll tell them how special they are when I can't find the words.

You pull on that sweater your mother knitted for you, wrapping my children, and me, in your warmth. Everybody knows of your power over restless toddlers, how you calm their overpowering fears with your quiet words. But did you know, Mr. Rogers, that while you nurture the young, you rescue their mothers on harrowing days when our tireless work has fallen short of the mark?

As the trolley tumbles down the track toward Make Believe, I, too, am caught in your web, searching, perhaps, for some clue from you that I am your friend and am special, too, despite all.

There you are, hanging up the sweater and pulling on your jacket, though I'm not yet ready for our visit to end. But as you wave good-bye, I realize the all the angry words I felt an hour ago are somehow missing from my mind. You smile at us, and I know that once again, you've worked magic in my house, soothing all the savage beasts that dwell here, most especially me.

Searching for Santa

Okay, I admit it. I'm thirty-seven years old, and I still believe in Santa Claus. I keep a picture of the Real Santa on my desk all year long. Next to the Christmas narrative in the Bible, the Polar Express is my favorite holiday book. And on Christmas morning, though I have recently conceded that the kids may go downstairs first, I always wake up wondering if this will be the year he'll visit me again.

When I was a child there were no Santas close to home. The Real Santa waited for Christmas in Richmond, sharing his Miller & Rhodes home with a beautiful Snow Queen and red-nosed Rudolph (kept quiet on the roof). Amid starlit bushes and flickering Christmas trees, thousands of children just like me came each year to watch the old elf climb down the chimney and to share their wishes on his velvet lap.

He looked the part, right down to his bulging middle and soft-as-powder beard. But Richmond's Santa possessed the magic of no other: He always knew my name.

Every visit, I'd wait my turn and watch, as one by one each child before me fell into Santa's magic. Child by child he spoke their names, though I couldn't help wondering, would he know me, too? My heart pounded as I reached the stage, but the Snow Queen, her white gown falling in soft drifts to the floor, always took a moment to calm me. Then Santa's face would appear from behind his chair, and he'd wink, calling my name in warm Tidewater tones that told me he would know me forever.

How could Santa *not* know you, this silent visitor who steals into your house while you sleep? He deftly leaves those gifts only you will treasure, giving you hope that someone really *knows* you, after all.

When I became a mother and moved to my husband's Atlanta hometown, I could think of no better Christmas gift to give my family than belief in Santa's magic. We took the kids downtown to visit a Big-City Santa, taking a ride on the Pink Pig, then standing in line for our turn in Santa's chair.

Our daughter, then just three, screamed as soon as Santa spoke to her. The baby drooled all over Santa's beard. I waited for the magic, for Santa to know their names like he had known mine. He chuckled and winked, ho-hoed and pinched a cheek, then it was on to the next child and another laundry list of wishes.

My heart ached for what seemed finally lost, even to me. Would my children ever know the real Santa Claus? If only we could go to Richmond.

No way, said the family Scrooge. Driving twelve hours just to see Santa was ridiculous; the kids would never miss what they didn't know.

But something was missing, and as each fall fell into winter, I grew more determined to share the gift of the Real Santa with my children.

When we moved home to North Carolina a few years later, the time had finally come.

We were up at dawn, the icy December rain slapping the house awake.

"All this, just for Santa Claus," Scrooge said from behind the wheel as we headed north on I-95, the wipers whining, too.

"Maybe it will change to snow," somebody said sleepily from the back seat. More growling from our driver, who'd lost his spirit years ago.

My husband's contempt comes from being raised in the city, where Santas are more plentiful than turkeys at holiday time. I paid him no mind, for soon he'd be cast in the magic I knew well.

I hadn't seen Santa in almost thirty years, and while I was excited, I was wary as well. This, too, could go the way of most childhood memories revisited; the spell could be broken in an instant if Santa didn't know my children. Without the magic, could I pretend for them?

But there we were, huddled in Richmond's City Market, waiting for our turn in Santa's gold-and-velvet chair. Babies slept in strollers, grand-parents read the morning paper, dads soothed anxious toddlers as the line wandered through the room like ribbon candy. We settled into our spots.

It seemed hours before we finally saw him, but with the first glimpse of his balding pink head, I knew I'd found my cherished friend after what felt like a lifetime of absence. Though the crow's feet were etched deeper into his face, his beard yellowed with age, he was still Santa, one hundred percent real.

As my children approached the Snow Queen, my heart began to pound until those thirty years had slipped away, and I was five again. He turned his twinkle toward their small frames, their eyes wide with wonder, then he spoke.

"Why, it's Meredith and Graham, all the way from Raleigh! Come on over here and tell me what you want for Christmas."

He knew, still. The bond was made, their belief—and mine—in Santa's magic firmly intact. Even Scrooge scratched his head in wonder.

It has been like this in Richmond for over forty years, as tens of thousands have shared in the magic of Richmond's Santa. Babies come in the company of cousins and mothers and grandfathers, aunts and uncles, many of whom have driven hundreds of miles and who just like me, spent hours as children waiting for one brief moment of magic.

And we keep coming back, most of us searching for our own Christmas memory—a treasured stocking filled with gum and tangerines, a half-eaten cookie, an empty bottle of Coke—magic that mall Santas don't give us, even on their best days.

For only in Richmond, Santa Claus shimmies down the chimney after his rooftop snack with Rudolph, watching as the line before him warms the room. And when it's your turn, his eyes peer over the back of his chair, and with a wink and a chuckle, he calls you over by name.

HAT CHECK

My mother had a hat to match every Sunday outfit: a wide-brimmed black hat with a crisp grosgrain bow, a red straw hat with netting for her face, and her favorite, a bright-blue cloche style covered with pink flowers and tiny green feathers that waved in the breeze. Each Sunday, be it winter or spring, she would delve deep into her closet through her neat hatbox stack, emerging, matched and stunning, ready for church in her best hat. She was beautiful, poised, reserved, and in control, her silver hair curling softly from beneath her chosen covering. Watching her from my place on the pew, she was all I ever dreamed of being—thin and beautiful and stunning in a hat.

I should have known I could never emulate my mother. The few hats I wore as a child all had elastic bands that pinched my chin. But I was silly, not sophisticated like my mother. Her hats were an extension of her personality, each one chosen carefully as a way for her, the mother of three young children, to show the world that despite our prickly heat, bandaged elbows and broken bones, she still had control. Just look at her hats.

I've always looked awful in hats. My hair is just short enough to be crushed beneath a brim, and my ears poke out just a little too far. That's not to say I don't have hats of my own. I actually have many more than my mother could ever dream of fitting into her small bedroom closet, but each one is invisible to the naked eye.

My self-portrait mirrors the drawing of the old man in a favorite children's book of mine, *Caps for Sale*. There I am with poked-out ears and googly eyes trying to balance a wobbly row of hats on my unkempt head, all of which have been thrown at me as if I'm a hat rack, standing empty and inviting.

On top is my mother hat, a hardhat, its shell stuffed with tissues, Band-Aids, and shrill-sounding whistles, should I need to be a nurse, referee, tutor, guidance counselor, fireman, handyman, construction worker, or any one of a host of other people, depending upon my children's momentary needs. Below the mother hat is a chauffeur's cap, under which I can be baseball coach, piano player, ambulance driver, or sports fan, depending, again, on moments and needs. Squeezed between them is the wife hat, which comes complete with its own "I-told-you-so" ribbon tied around its brim, a honey-do list waving like Minnie Pearl's price tag, and an alarm clock, should I fall asleep before my husband's flight gets in. This hat, which doubles as a teleprompter screen to remind me how to conduct adult conversation, is a must for nights out at the movies and dinner with friends.

Scattered in the pile are a dozen other styles for when I need to be a daughter, sister, neighbor or friend, and a "don't-mess-with-me" Stetson I keep on the kitchen counter at supper in case one of those annoying telemarketers should call. Somewhere far below them all is my writer's hat, a tiny pillbox, which I never really ever take off, but which can only be seen in those rare moments when all the other hats are unoccupied.

Not being a one-hat-at-a-time kind of person, I usually have several hats fighting for headspace at once. My chef's hat creates a meal at the stove while I talk on the phone with the help of my business hat and prepare a snack for the kids in my short-order cook hat, my writer's hat constantly feeding me with first lines of stories it wishes I'd write.

(Perhaps I'll get a secretary hat to write them all down.) But you won't find my unworn hats tucked neatly away in boxes. They are likely strewn across the kitchen counter, waiting for someone responsible, like my mother, to put them away.

I daydream of being a magician, top hat in hand, trying to pull one hat out of the pile to wear alone without all the others spilling onto the floor. Every now and then, I can do it, though on most days, my hat stack tips and sways like the deck of a ship in stormy weather. A few stay put, but many fall, and I scramble to put them back in place before anyone notices I'm not managing.

Despite my varied collection, I still lack that one hat to give me the poise provided by my mother's feathered cloche. Perhaps it's because I've never been in control of my life as my mother was of hers. Or maybe, as I'd rather think, she really wore all the same hats I do, but she just used her favorite, feathered one to hide them all.

Eleven-Day Weekend

Blame it on wishful thinking. Maybe this year, I told the kids, just maybe we'll get a little snow. A weekend dusting would be nice, enough to pull out the sled, throw a day's worth of snowballs, build a fort. Just enough to cover the ground and be melted in time for school on Monday.

No matter that my children had never seen more than a couple of inches of snow at one time. I can remember when things were different, when the white stuff provided days of sledding and snow cream and no school, and I was hopeful. It was bound to happen again.

Well, let's just say we've made this memory and it's time to move on. We've been sledding, so much now that the runners on our plastic sleds have worn through and now double as snow scoopers when sliding down icy cul-de-sacs. We've made chili, hot chocolate and corn bread, stoked fires, played blackjack, watched *Apollo 13* at least thirteen times, caught flakes on our eyelids, bundled and rebundled ourselves until we are really very weary of it all.

And there has not been an hour in the last six days when the dryer wasn't running.

Funny, I don't ever remember tiring of snow before, but I wasn't the mother then. All I cared about was waxing my sled's runners and having to share it too often with my sister. Now there's a constant puddle at the back door, soaked gloves lined up by the fire, and I really, really want to mop the kitchen floor.

As I write this, rumor has it that the weather may turn again, and if that happens, my son says, we'll have spent an eleven-day weekend together, thanks to a planned two-day school holiday next week.

I suppose that's what it seems like to him, a perpetual weekend. Sleeping late, pancakes for breakfast, cartoons and homemade hot chocolate, movies in the late afternoon, no homework, no having to put on the good shoes for church.

And it's not just the kids. Dear Dad, who was supposed to fly to the Northeast this week, has enjoyed getting to know Regis over his coffee in the morning. By afternoon, he's taking to the slopes, exhibiting sledding prowess unmatched by those half his age.

But "we" have had to make the coffee and clean up all those chocolate-soaked mugs and the leftover popcorn kernels, the same "we" who fills (and empties) the dryer and folds the clothes and builds the fire and slides to the store for more milk to make more hot chocolate, because you wouldn't want to run out. I mean, it's cold outside.

Right now, as seven days at home begin to melt into eight, the prospect of another four with my adorable, loving family is almost too much to contemplate. Don't get me wrong. It was a great holiday, with music and lights and yeast rolls and good company, but that was way back in December, and now it's January. Time to get back to normal.

But a winter thaw won't bring enough heat to melt my family back into their appointed corners of the world soon enough. I'm feeling desperate, unable to find space in my house where someone isn't watching something or piling something wet in the middle of the floor or asking what's for the next meal. No, we need real heat, the scorching mid-July kind, complete with gnats and mosquitoes, to light a fire under my crew.

I can see it now, so hot they'll want to sleep late, and if they do venture outside, they'll pour back in, dripping their sweaty clothes onto the floor. They'll need something cool to drink, to take a shower—I mean it'll be so hot outside. And after they leave their wet bath towels on the floor, they're bound to go searching for that copy of *Apollo 13*.

Hmm ….

More snow you say? Bring it on: We have our escape all planned. We'll hit the slopes, capture flakes on our noses, and build a fort if we feel like it.

And since they tired of it all during the first half of our eleven-day weekend, my family should have plenty of time to have the chocolate piping hot, the dryer going, when I (I mean "we") are ready to come in from the cold.

SPIRIT OF CHRISTMAS PASSED

As Garth Brooks pleads with me to have myself a merry little Christmas, I pass a line of pickup trucks towing a parade of holiday floats along U.S. 64. No way that's real snow beneath Santa's sleigh. I check the temperature—75 degrees—and scan the cotton fields nearby expecting to find palm trees instead of pine.

Garth drones on, and I can't help wishing somebody would write a new Christmas song. The old ones seem as tired as I am of the holiday, and it isn't even here yet. The radio, the TV, the sidewalks at the mall all scream Christmas. My neighbors have set out their lawn lights, lit window candles, and hung their wreaths. But I've yet to bring out a single scrap of Christmas cheer.

Maybe it's the weather.

I dread dragging out the ornaments, untangling the lights, checking my tired old list to see whom I've forgotten. I always write a tongue-in-cheek holiday newsletter, but this year I have writer's block. I have done a little shopping, only because December hit without my putting a single dollar into the Christmas economy, and I felt guilty. This year shopping feels like just another chore.

This from someone who believed in the possibility of Santa long after my children stopped. Whatever happened to the me who used to stay up late making yeast rolls for all the neighbors, who took delight in singing Christmas carols to my kids as they snuggled into bed?

Now that my children are practically grown, much of what made Christmas so magical is missing. We don't scatter reindeer food on the ground outside the house anymore; we even forget to leave a hot yeast roll and some eggnog for Santa. We used to read aloud the Christmas story from the Book of Luke and *The Polar Express*, but somehow we put those traditions aside, too. Now we come in from midnight services and shoo the kids off to their rooms, knowing they hear us as we sleepily stuff the stockings full.

After all those years of making magic for everyone else, I want someone to make it for me. But no one can. And I keep thinking of all the children who lost their parents on September 11, of friends battling cancer, of all the children whose lives are split apart by war, and I'm ashamed of myself for wanting more than I feel like giving.

I know I should celebrate all that's good in my life. Publishing a book and launching a regular newspaper column in the past year, good kids who stay out of trouble, a husband who loves me, parents who are strong and healthy—all this should be enough when so many around me suffer so much more than seasonal malaise. I know all this—and still I resent the Cratchits of the world for their ability to celebrate the simple joy around them.

There are just some days when the kids fall short, when my husband can't read my mind, when the next career goal seems so unsure that I just don't feel like looking for the Christmas in my life. Selfish, sure, but it's hard to muster up the sparkle when I know it's not in one of the boxes of ornaments I've yet to unpack.

I long for the days when I could find the perfect gift in the toy aisles. But life—and Christmas—seem much more complicated these days. I've reached the age when what my family wants most can't be found on Santa's list. Their wish—to be accepted for who they are—is something they must give themselves.

Seems I've forgotten, too, that what made the season shine for me was my own belief in it. I hope I can find where I packed it away before Christmas comes and goes without me.

Mapping It Out

The plane leaves the ground, the giant trucks on the runway becoming Matchbox cars, and I watch the land below me transform itself into a map. I forget this about flying, how the earth really does become a map, how lights far below me blink like cat eyes in the twilight, how rivers really do resemble snakes.

As I watch, I can't help but think about that truth of marriage: one spouse reads maps and the other doesn't. My husband can barely unfold the map before frustration hits, but I study them. We head out somewhere, and I make note of the route, the rivers we'll cross, add up the miles and the hours. We joke that this is why he keeps me around.

In turn, I am the one who minds the family map, finding our destination and setting the course. I keep the calendars, make the appointments, and balance the checkbook, so the four of us stay on target.

Lately, though, it seems the map itself has taken over as I move through days encumbered by details. The college applications that loom, the appointments I have to make (and remember.) The house, the husband, the children who are only home long enough lately to touch base, yet still need the base—all wrangle for my direction and attention. Not to mention the job.

I'm expected to be in control of everything, when I have never felt more out of it. I show up half an hour late for appointments, lose my glasses over and over, and I haven't balanced the checkbook in two months. I am that river I see below me, slowing down as it hits the flatlands, spreading out into an alluvial fan, with a multitude of streamlets flowing out from first this bend then the next—so many outlets that I feel soon I'll come up empty of the water that defines me.

I heard a sermon recently about the disease of "busy-ness," and I know I have it. I am so entangled in my life that I often fail to *see* the map I've laid out for myself. I hardly reach one destination when I think of where else I need to go next, who else needs me for what. My kids grab my shoulders and say, "Mom! Are you listening?" Too often I'm not.

If only I could find a moment when there is no next, maybe then I could enjoy being where I am. Just a moment, really. That would surely bring a cure.

———

We land in New York City, and using a book of maps, we comb the streets, catch a couple of shows, fight the crowds on Broadway. The kids try to take in that MTV show they like, but our timing is off. When night falls, they cringe at the thought of all four of us staying in one room. Teenagers need their privacy, but the budget doesn't allow that this trip.

I wake up in the middle of the night, aware of my husband's snores, my son's sleeping gibberish, my daughter's soft breathing. I think of my son, who has grown to be six feet tall and remember when he barely reached my skirts. Though his toes stretch far over the end of the bed these days, he still hugs me each morning as he heads out to school and spills his day to me when he walks in the door at its end.

This may be one of the last trips we take with my daughter, seventeen now, who has her sights focused on college. Though she is like her father and hates maps of any kind, lately she's been marking her own path, one that will soon lead her outside the margins of my own. I marvel at her clear smile, how she has become the young woman I longed to be at her age, so beautiful, poised, and happy.

My husband's snoring, usually the noise that keeps me awake, becomes, on this night far away from home, a sort of melody, and instead of tapping him, I lie quietly and listen to its rhythms, remembering the history, the map I've traveled with him in our twenty years together. I know that in just a few years, it will be just the two of us at home, and I'm hoping when that happens, we will be at the same point in the road.

Though I can hear the sirens and the cab horns splitting the night in the world's busiest city, somehow I know I've found my moment, that the map has brought me here, away from the noise of my life, so I can hear what I've been missing. I'm thankful now for this small moment when I can fly above it all and really see the map again, reset my course, knowing how important where I've been is to where I'm headed next.

Author Mom

There are days when my son wishes I had a normal job, say that of an SBI agent. It's not fair, he says, that because writing chose me when I was twelve, his teachers expect him to write well, too.

It's bad enough for your mom tell the neighbors all your shortcomings. But I've shared my children's foibles in the newspaper, for even strangers to see. (They really aren't as bad as I've made them out to be.)

And now I had to go and write a book.

It's a real book that cracks when you open it, the pages smooth and white and filled with thousands of words strung together like jewels. Or at least that's how it looks to me.

But my kids don't share my fascination. They're still recovering from the creation of it. It took up residence in our house almost three years ago and, like a whining toddler, required way too much of my attention.

I'll probably have to pay them to read it because it's history and that's too much like school. They won't even wear the T-shirts I bought them, the back filled with the names of authors and their books (mine included) because the front says "Can't Live Without Books," and they so easily think they can.

At least it's not about them.

I actually thought the timing was good, having two teenagers who could do laundry if asked, make a grilled cheese, scramble an egg. But they had other needs.

Mom, can you . . .? Mom, have you seen . . .? Mom, can I . . .? I met their questions with a stare: No, Mom hasn't. No Mom can't right now. Mom's writing a book, remember? Oh, that.

But just wait until it's done, and I'll make a really nice dinner, do the laundry, clean the house. Go back to "momming" again. When did I leave it?

In the last year especially, they've seen me typing, always typing, on the phone too much, crying when my computer crashed. What kind of fun job is that? They probably didn't believe I was creating, trying to fashion myself into the author I'd dreamed of being when they were still a twinkle in God's eye. Did Hemingway stop in the middle of *The Old Man and the Sea* to run to the grocery store before making dinner?

They couldn't feel, as I could, when it all came together, when it felt like a book.

"I'll be glad when you're finished," my daughter said, about a month before it was actually done. "Then you can be a normal mom again."

Surely they know by now that I will never really be that.

I didn't always write. They've forgotten when they were small, when together we painted with watercolors, when their easel, not my computer, was a permanent fixture. Or when homemade cookies weren't Slice 'n' Bake.

And all those days we sat, reading books that weren't mine. They couldn't see then that I was dreaming.

When I did start to write again, they were part of it. They entangled themselves in the phone cord once while I was conducting an interview. (Having scheduled it during *Sesame Street*, I thought I was safe.) I wrote about them and their wonderful entanglement in my life.

In the last year, they've celebrated the joys with me, high-fiveing me when the acceptance letter came, taking my picture when the completed manuscript finally left the house.

When the box of books arrived two weeks ago, my daughter carefully thumbed through the pages with me, commenting on this and that. Later, she took my picture again. I could tell she was pleased and maybe understood some of what it took to get to this very big moment, huge in my life, though not even close to the winter days she and her brother were born.

I hope, now that it's done, that they understand the importance of finding that something that moves them, apart from family and friends, and of dreaming and stretching themselves until it changes their world, if only for a little while.

They're coming around. Just yesterday they decided to make their own T-shirt that says, "My mom wrote a book about the beach." With luck the Cliffs Notes will be out before someone asks them what it's all about.

MOTHER WORDS

Mothers cradle and they rock.
They coach and they soothe,
Aggravate and persist,
Sing and celebrate,
Praise and punish,
Meddle and forgive.

Mothers hope and they mourn.
They confuse and they cheer,
Scold and brag,
Spoil and surprise,
Inspect and apologize.
Mothers worry.

Mothers pray and they mourn.
They plant and they believe,
Provoke and protect,
Bandage and bend,
Push and pick up,
Mothers cope.

And they bathe us
in their love without ceasing,
They give us room
to breathe.

Children cuddle and they coo.
Children reach and they console,
Annoy and prevail,
Challenge and accept,
Inspire and emulate,
Pray and pretend.

Children play and they create,
They celebrate and they whine.
Tickle and rebel,
Inspect and energize,
Climb and inquire,
Children dance.

Children giggle and they grieve.
They doubt and make believe,
Dream and disappoint,
Struggle and soar,
Hide and seek,
Children hope.

And they love without ceasing.
when we give them room
to breathe.

sbr, 2003

AUTHOR BIOGRAPHY

Susan Byrum Rountree is a writer, wife, and mother whose life's work centers on the small ceremonies of daily life. A former newspaper columnist, she is the author of *Nags Headers*, a narrative history set on North Carolina's Outer Banks, which won the Willie Parker Peace History Book Award in 2001 and was nominated as the Southeast Booksellers Non-fiction Book of the Year that same year.

She lives in Raleigh, North Carolina with her family and is currently at work on a novel.

To learn more about the author
or to order additional copies
of *In Mother Words*, visit
www.susanbyrumrountree.com.